know your
HAMSTER

Earl Schneider, editor

THE PET LIBRARY LTD

THE PET LIBRARY LTD ®

The Pet Library Ltd, sub-
sidiary of Sternco Indus-
tries, Inc., 600 South
Fourth Street, Harrison,
N.J. Exclusive Canadian
Distributor: Hartz Moun-
tain Pet Supplies Limited,
1125 Talbot Street, St.
Thomas,Ontario,Canada.

Exclusive United Kingdom
Distributor: The Pet Library
(London) Ltd, 30 Borough
High Street, London S.E.1.

PRINTED IN THE NETHERLANDS

1 2 3 4 5 6 7 8 9 10

ISBN 0-87826-754-9

CONTENTS

1   What is a hamster?

He is a charming little animal with a twinkling nose and black eyes and resembles, some say, a tiny bear; and others, a chipmunk, field mouse, or monkey. That he looks like a cross between a large mouse and a small guinea pig is perhaps the most apt comparison. When fully grown, the Golden Hamster is between five and six inches long, red-gold in color, and, unlike his cousins the rats and mice, has only a tiny stub of a tail. This last, undoubtedly, has played a large part in his popularity: a pet rat or mouse's most objectionable feature is his long tail.

Although hamsters were first introduced into this country in 1938 as experimental laboratory animals, they did not become generally known to pet-fanciers until after World War II, and it was not until 1947 that they first took the pet world by storm. Today, less than twenty years later, there are in this country alone, at least seven million of them, not to mention Great Britain where they are just as popular, and the rest of the world.

And it all began in 1930 with one mother and a litter of twelve baby hamsters which a zoologist, Professor I. Aharoni of Hebrew University in Jerusalem, found in the Syrian desert near the town of Aleppo. Syria is a country at the far end of the Mediterranean Sea, to the north of Israel. Exploring the desert, Professor Aharoni came upon a mother hamster and her litter deep in an underground burrow. By the time he got his tiny family back to his laboratory in Jerusalem, however, all but three of them had died or escaped. These three, however, continued in excellent health and within four months the first litter of golden hamsters ever to be born in captivity was delivered.

As they matured, these babies were interbred, and as the now tame hamsters multiplied they were used in research experiments. Soon they began to attract widespread attention in the scientific world. Because these hamsters were so disease-free and because they bred so rapidly—it is possible for them to have a litter once a month—and because they were so docile and easy to handle, they came to be highly regarded as research animals and their fame spread quickly throughout the world.

This is what happens when a young lady is turned loose in a commercial hamstery and told to select an occupant for her cage. Notice how the front portion of each drawer is slanted for ventilation. The cards tacked on the fronts are record cards where the breeder records such important facts as parentage, dates of birth, number in litter, etc.

SALLY ANNE THOMPSON
For the moment the lovely Amber-gold male seems to be the choice.

From Jerusalem, scientists took them to laboratories in France, Britain and, in 1938, to the United States. All present-day golden hamsters in captivity, including all the various colors, with the exception of a few brought back from Syria by travelers and military personnel, are the descendants of that first tiny family found by Professor Aharani.

For the scientifically minded, the golden hamster's correct name is *Mesocricetus auratus auratus,* usually shortened to *Cricetus auratus.* It is commonly referred to as the Syrian Golden Hamster to distinguish it from two of its relatives, the European or Black Hamster, and the Chinese or Gray Hamster. The name hamster is derived from the German word *hamstern* meaning "to hoard". It was bestowed on Cricetus because of his peculiar habit of filling two expandible pouches on the sides of his head with all the food he can stow there, and then, when he thinks he is not being observed slipping away to hide it, thus living up to his name of Hoarder.

The European or Black Hamster (*Cricetus cricetus*) and the Chinese or Gray Hamster (*Cricetus griseus*) should not be confused with the Golden Hamster. Neither of them have been tamed for pets. The Chinese Hamster ranges from China to the Caspian Sea between Europe and Asia. The European hamster ranges from the western coasts to a point roughly north of India. Where these two ranges overlap, the Syrian or Golden Hamster is found. Its range is much more limited than the Black and Gray, and it appeared, apparently, much later in evolutionary history. It is the "middle-sized" hamster which is what *Mesocricetus* means compared to the European which is about nine inches long and the Chinese which is four or five. The Chinese Hamster is gray above with a black stripe down the center of its back, and light below. The European hamster is light brown above, black below, and white at the sides. Both are sometimes used for food, and their skins for coat linings.

In countries where they are common, the farmers do not only harvest their own fields, they dig into the hamsters' granaries as well. In each burrow they find a storage bin which may hold anywhere from 30 to 60 pounds of grain which the hamsters have stored up for the winter.

Appearance of the hamster

If some people think the Golden Hamster resembles a tiny bear, it is easy to see why when he rears up on his hind legs and dances around. His hair is dense and sleek, reddish-gold in color on the back while the belly side is a greyish-white. This hair is sparse when compared to the fur on the upper side of the body. The head, once narrow and rat-like, has grown broader and shorter with selective breeding. There are black markings on his head and cheeks while across the chest runs a broad band of dark fur.

The forelegs each possess four toes and a rudimentary thumb. This causes their charming resemblance to tiny baby hands. But their feet are well adapted for digging and climbing and they have sharp claws. The five digits on the back feet are fully developed. The strong muscles of the hindlegs enable the hamster to crawl backward as well as forward through the narrow passages of his native burrow. His short legs give him a walking movement which can only be described as a waddle.

The eyes are bold and limpid, black in color. The ears are large, erect, dark colored, but with almost no hair. The tail is almost, but not quite, missing, being about a third of an inch long. Flesh colored, it is sparsely covered with short white hair.

The hamster has a voice too. The babies squeal as they scamper around and yap when they are nipped. Their mother croons them to sleep with a kind of hamster lullaby.

But the hamster's most fascinating feature is, of course, his cheek pouches into which he can stuff a truly incredible amount of food. When his pouches are full, and his head ballooned to double its size, he resembles no other animal in the world. These pouches are located on the sides of his head, neck and shoulders, right under the dark stripes. They have no connection with his digestive organs. When relaxed, they are about an inch deep but when crammed with food they extend another inch at least. This unbelievable stretching power has caused many owners on first seeing their new pets' pouches full to phone the vet to announce that their hamsters had mumps!

When he wants to empty his pouches, the hamster simply leans forward and pushes on them with his tiny hands,

But then this Piebald or spotted male takes her fancy. This is a hard decision to make.

SALLY ANNE THOMPSON
He certainly seems affectionate, but perhaps a little too lively.

depositing the hoarded treasure in some favored hiding place. Just as the hamster's pouches will stretch, so will his skin. It fits loosely over his whole body as if it were too big for him. In fact, it is too big. It can be pulled out as far as an inch without causing him any great discomfort.

The hamster being a member of the rodent family is well equipped with gnawing teeth. He also has strong jaws to help him gnaw. The teeth are somewhat unique: they have no roots. They extend far in to the jaw and grow out at a rate that approximates the rate of wear resulting from their constant eating and gnawing. In fact, since a hamster's teeth never stop growing it is important that he be given hardwood or bones to gnaw on to keep his teeth from growing right on out of his head. There are four rodent-like incisor teeth to cut with as well as molars to grind the food. Only the fronts of the teeth are enameled. This means that the backs wear out more quickly. The remaining enamel forms a sharp cutting edge which the hamster uses to gnaw roots, wood, and other tough material.

Differentiation between males and females is not difficult. Looking down on them, the male's body is elongated, presenting a tapered rear view, while the rear of the female is more blunt and not as brightly colored as that of the male. The female, too, is usually larger and heavier than the male, averaging about a half inch longer and a half ounce heavier.

Color variation

Markings are consistent on all Golden Hamsters but color variations are being seen more and more as a result of mutations and selective breeding. Those most commonly seen are the Albino, the Piebald, sometimes called Panda or Harlequin, and the Amber-Gold. They differ in color only; not in size or in conformation.

Albino: All white except for his ears and nose which are black, and his eyes which are pink or ruby-red. He sometimes suffers from defective vision. This is because his pink eyes are highly sensitive to light. None of the hamsters, however, have very good sight because they are all nocturnal animals—creatures of the night.

Piebald or Panda: Golden with white spotting, but the amount of spotting varies. He has a temperament to match his exotic beauty and is not too easily tamed.

Amber-Gold or Cinnamon: Also called Champagne, was discovered in 1958. Amber or fawn colored fur, dark red eyes and light colored ears.

There are other color varieties and mutants too, and we discuss them later in this book in the section *Genetics of Hamster Breeding.*

All of these varieties are, of course, higher in price than the common Golden Hamster because of their relative rarity.

Choosing your hamster

When buying a hamster or any other pet it is always wise to go to a reputable pet shop or breeder. Do not try to look for bargains. Good hamsters are not that expensive. Nor should you buy from a private party unless you know what you're getting. An untamed or badly tamed hamster can only result in disappointment, and there is always the possibility that an unknown hamster may be ill-tempered because of bad treatment. The wisest procedure is to select a healthy young animal and train it yourself.

Look for one between five and eight weeks old. Baby hamsters are very shy and easily frightened so it is useless to attempt to tame one until he's a little, but not too much, older. You should also remember that the hamster's natural life-span is only about two to three years, and you will be able to enjoy yours for a longer time if you get him soon after he's been weaned.

Pet shops vary in the way they keep and display hamsters. Keeping them in individual cages is undoubtedly the best way but some shops do not always do this, keeping their younger animals altogether in a collective cage. It is preferable not to choose a hamster from a cage containing both sexes of unknown age. You may end up with a pregnant female.

SALLY ANNE THOMPSON

She clasps her hands to prevent a fall. Hamsters seem oblivious to the danger in heights, perhaps because they are normally ground-dwelling animals.

And this is her final choice: a Golden Hamster who shows his acceptance by calmly eating from her hand.

Take your time. Ask the dealer to show you as many animals as you want to look at. You'll want to make sure that your choice is in good physical condition with an even-going disposition. Care now may very well prevent problems later on.

First look for all around signs of friendliness and good health—soft sleek fur, bright clear eyes, and a general feel of solidity. Avoid bony or skinny animals.

Look at the ears. They will give you a good idea of the hamster's age. In a young hamster, the insides of the ears are covered with tiny white hairs. These gradually disappear with age and when the animal is older the ears are hairless and shiny.

After examining the ears, look at his nose, feet and belly. There should be no pimples or blemishes. These are the signs of mange. If you find an animal with a runny nose or watery eyes, or one whose movements are lethargic, avoid him too. A wet tail is also a sign of poor health. Make sure there are no scars or bald patches in his fur.

You may, however, accept small spots on the hips. These will be about the same size as the hamster's eyes and feel much thicker than the rest of the skin. These are called dimorphic pigment spots and are perfectly normal. Although they usually develop on older animals, they are *not* necessarily an indicator of age.

Some may have nicks in their ears. There is always the possibility that the ears have been bitten in a tussle; however, it is far more possible that these are just breeder's marks, used by him to identify his hamsters much like brands are used to identify cattle. These marks have no ill effects.

How many? This, of course, is a matter of your requirements. Do you want to breed hamsters or do you want just one as a pet?

Since they are by nature solitary animals, there is no need to worry that one will be lonely by himself. If he gets a reasonable amount of affection from his owner, he will be perfectly happy to live alone.

If you do want more than one hamster, remember that they cannot be housed together in the same cage, except for purposes of breeding, after they are eight weeks old.

Male or female? Sex isn't too important if you decide on only one animal. The females have a tendency to grow less friendly as they get older whereas males are more likely to remain docile. A pregnant female may be a bit more snappish; however this is true of the females of most species.

If you do pick a female, check her carefully to make sure that she is not pregnant. Ask the dealer to determine this for you. Of course, if she is nearly ready to litter, her condition will be fairly obvious. A less prominent bulge in her stomach can be detected by comparing her with other nearby females.

Don't choose a hamster just be observing him in his cage. Have the dealer take him out of the cage and place him on a counter or table where you can get a closer look. Do not, of course, try to take the hamster out of the cage yourself but observe carefully how the seller does it. Is he nervous and squeamish about handling the animal? Take this as a negative sign.

After the hamster has been placed on the table, do not try to pick him up. Give him a chance to become acquainted with you, perhaps by offering him some tidbit. The chances are excellent that the inquisitiveness for which hamsters are noted will bring him to you in a hurry.

Once he seems to be accustomed to you, extend your hand slowly and offer him the tidbit. Remember that he is still nervous so do not make any sudden moves.

If the hamster does not scurry away from your out-stretched hand, let it hover over him for a moment so that he sees it, then close it gently but firmly around his entire body so that it is cradled in your closed fist. Never reach down from above and suddenly pick up a hamster. You are almost sure to be nipped. Some owners prefer to pick up their pets by bringing their hands together, palms up, on either side of their hamster and then scoop him up into their open hands.

When you have picked him up successfully, inspect him for the points we have just discussed. If he is difficult to pick up, seems afraid or tries to bite, select another animal and follow the same procedure.

This is a Black-eared or semi-Albino male. It is not a true Albino because there is some pigment in the ears.

SALLY ANNE THOMPSON

An Albino female. All pigmentation is lacking. Even the eyes are actually colorless. The red you see is the blood circulating in the capillaries behind them.

3   Housing

The hamster does not require a great deal of maintenance. But the few things he does need are essential, and great pains should be taken to make sure that he gets them.

There are many types of cages designed especially for hamsters which can be purchased at pet shops and variety store pet counters. Some are elaborate and expensive but many can be purchased at a reasonable price, and these are recommended unless you have the time and skill to build your own.

The most convenient of the mass-produced cages are those made of metal resembling a bird cage. They are equipped with a sliding bottom which greatly facilitates their cleaning. They come in various sizes; get the largest cage that you can afford. The hamster is an active little creature who likes to move around. He will become nervous and snappish if he is kept for long in a cage which is too small for him because he will not get enough exercise.

I prefer a cage that is at least 24 in. long, 18 in. deep and 12 in. high. There is on the market one excellent cage which is not only large enough, it is built with two levels, with a small staircase leading from the lower to the higher. Its only disadvantage is that it is a little more difficult to clean.

The cage should be deeply padded with a good absorbent material. You may use wood shavings, a commercially prepared hamster litter, or even several thicknesses of newspaper. Cedar shavings are best but most hamsters prefer newspaper. They enjoy shredding it. Avoid any bedding material which might irritate or lacerate cheek pouches. Never use old woollen blankets or other fabrics to line a hamster's cage. He will chew and swallow them, upsetting his digestion. Moreover, the fabric will quickly become wet and dirty, and it will not be as easy to dispose of as newspaper or shavings.

Next you will need a feeding dish and a hamster water bottle. The feeding dish need not be too large, but it should be fastened securely to the side of the cage so that it cannot be knocked over. It should be accessible from the outside so that it will not be necessary to open the cage every time you want to feed your pet.

The water bottle is necessary because the hamsters will quickly make a mess of their cage if water is given to them in an open dish. Such a water bottle can be bought at pet shops or you can make your own by taking a small bottle and fitting it with a rubber cork. Through this cork insert a curved bit of glass or plastic tubing. Fill the bottle, plug the cork in firmly, and hang it upside down on the outside of the cage with the curved tip of the tube penetrating inside. A drop will form at the tip and will remain there until the hamster licks it off, then another drop will form, and so on.

To make sure that your pet gets plenty of exercise, try to find a cage equipped with a wire exercise wheel. If not, buy a wheel and install it yourself. Another fun and exercise device is a slide which your hamster will enjoy tremendously providing a little added amusement for you. Hamsters love to play with these devices, and the exercise is good for them.

Building a cage

If you decide to build your own cage, there are several things to bear in mind. For one, the hamster is a gnawing animal, and he will gnaw through a wooden cage unless it is strongly built and reinforced with wire netting. Use at least $\frac{5}{8}$ in. hardwood for the floor, back and sides, and wire mesh for the top and front.

The cage should be approximately 24 in. long, 12 in. high, and 12 in. from back to front. A hinged trap-door can be cut into one of the ends; or, if preferred, the entire mesh-covered top can be made into a hinged lid, with a catch to keep it closed.

Paint the whole inside with a non-toxic paint; this helps to discourage gnawing. Paint the outside any attractive color you desire.

The wooden floor should be lined with metal. This will insure that the hamster cannot gnaw his way out, and it makes the floor that much easier to keep clean. A flat metal pan, like a cookie sheet, can be used for this purpose; it can be easily removed for cleaning. Such a pan will prevent droppings and stored food and water dripping from penetrating the bottom of the cage to cause odor.

A sleeping chamber or nest not less than 6 inches square should be placed inside the cage. This too should be of metal

Male Golden Hamster: this is the original color variety. All other colors were bred from the Golden.

A group of Blue hamsters. This is a new color and has not yet been fully accepted.

with a removable top to make cleaning easier. If you do not give your hamster such a little house, make sure he has plenty of straw or shavings in which to hide whenever he feels like it. Excelsior, hay or shredded paper can also be used for nesting material.

If you have a good-sized bird cage around that is not in use, it can be made to serve as a hamster cage. Be sure that the bars are close enough together to prevent his squeezing his head through. Remove the softwood perches to prevent his gnawing them, but replace one or two of them with whittled sticks of hardwood.

A glass aquarium tank can be used for hamsters too, with minor adaptions. A wire-mesh lid will have to be fitted to the top, and at least one of the glass sides replaced with wire netting to give the hamster an exercise wall. It is for this reason that solid glass jars are not recommended except as temporary homes. All hamsters need wire netting to climb on.

Your hamster should always have a beef or ham bone to chew on, or a branch of hardwood, or fruitwood, to nibble at. This will not only help to keep his teeth clean, it will keep them worn down to their proper length.

If you have reason to believe that your pet's claws have grown too long, they can be clipped with manicure scissors or nail clippers. Be careful not to cut into the quick, the blood vessel that runs down the center of each claw.

When selecting a spot in which to set up the cage, choose one that is warm and free of drafts. It should be in a room with a relatively constant temperature otherwise the hamster is likely to catch cold. Remember also that the hamster is a nocturnal animal. Given his choice he will sleep during the day and begin his activities after the sun has gone down. If the temperature drops too much at night, he will not feel like moving around, and may even hibernate.

Because he is nocturnal, the hamster's cage should be kept in a dark corner so that he can rest during the day. Do not keep the cage in the sun. The hamster's eyes are not designed for exposure to strong light so if you keep his cage in a bright spot you will seldom see him because he will stay hidden in his nest or buried in the shavings.

Care of the cage

The hamster's cage should be cleaned thoroughly at least once a week. One of the all-purpose cleaners like Lestoil with a pine scent is good for this. It will help keep down odors.

When you clean the cage, you will find stored-away food. Remove some, especially if it is rotting, but not all because this will upset him and he will rush around the cage for some time looking for it. Replace it in the spot you found it. This is true too of the little wads of bedding that you will find. Put them back after each cleaning. The hamster doesn't like having to make his bed any more than you do, and he will be greatly annoyed if he has to begin all over again.

The hamster's droppings, which are hard and dry, will be left in one area. A corner of the cage as far from the nest as possible will be used for urination. This corner should be cleaned out each day and new litter added. Some owners solve this problem by using a large jar with a mouth wide enough for the hamster to enter. They lay this jar on its side in the corner of the cage which the hamster prefers for urination. He will use this jar for his toilet, and the floor of the cage will stay dry. The jar should be washed out daily and replaced when it becomes stained.

Make sure that his feeding dish is kept scrupulously clean. The water bottle should be washed out each day by flushing it with fresh water.

Temperature

Hamsters should be kept in a room with a temperature between 55 and 70°F. Adult hamsters can stand considerably lower temperatures, but the newborn hamster cannot. A drop of temperature to 45°F. will cause him to go into a state of hibernation. He will sleep, the body will become rigid, and its temperature will fall below normal. If this should happen to your hamster do not make the mistake that many novice owners have of destroying their pet because they thought he was dead. Gentle warming will usually "thaw" him out. See the treatment recommended under *Health*.

Cream hamster. The eyes and ears are dark.

This cage is just big enough for one hamster.

This little fellow almost seems lost in his cage but in time he'll grow. The water in the bottle in the corner is kept from running out by air pressure. The hamster licks the water from the tube at the bottom. Chromium-plated hamster cages are easier to keep clean.

4   Feeding your hamster

Feeding a hamster is no great problem. He will eat just about anything. Commercially prepared hamster food is available at most pet shops and will supply the vitamins and minerals that your hamster needs to stay healthy. It comes in pellet form and it should be used as the staple element of your pet's daily ration.

If such food is not available, or if you run short, you may substitute poultry grain, kibbled dog or cat food, bird seed, dry bread, or breakfast cereal temporarily, but you should return to the prepared food as soon as possible. A one-pound package of this will keep the average hamster supplied for about a month.

As to fresh fruit and vegetables, go easy on them. While your hamster needs some of the vitamins they contain, they should not be fed more often than once or twice a week. Carrots, cabbage, or lettuce can be offered for this. Grapes and apple bits are all right too providing the apple contains no rotten spots. These can prove fatal.

Avoid as much as possible any foods containing a high percentage of water. This is true, too, of milk. While milk is very good for hamsters and contributes greatly to their growth, it is dangerous when it begins to turn sour. Feed them dry milk, making sure that no moisture touches it.

The main reason for feeding only dry food is the hamster's habit of storing it away. Moist foods decay and generate harmful bacteria.

According to the US Department of Agriculture's study of the hamster's vitamin requirements, A, D, E, and K, and some of the B group are essential. Lack of vitamin E will result in death in 4 to 18 weeks. So check any prepared food which you may purchase for its content of these vitamins. An adult hamster will require about half an ounce of food each day.

The important thing to remember is that, like yourself, your pet will want variety in his diet. Even though the commercial foods are excellent, pamper your pet at times by giving him a treat of sunflower seeds or fresh fruit. It will make taming and training your pet easier if you use these treats as rewards.

At feeding time the hamster is an entertaining performer. He will scurry over to the feeding dish to inspect the bill of fare, then he will begin to stuff the food into his cheek pouches. When his head has expanded to about twice its size, he will disappear with his treasure to unload it wherever he has his hoard hidden. As soon as he has disposed of the first load he will return for another.

When he has finished, the hamster will come out of his nest and stand at the door brushing his nose with his little hands and grooming himself like a cat. He prefers to eat without an audience and will do so later at his own convenience. All he cares about at first is gathering up as much food as he can and storing it away.

It is amusing to watch the hamster stuffing his cheek pouches and this leads to the temptation of feeding him often. No harm in this. No matter how much food you supply him with, he will not overeat. He is by nature a frugal animal. Nor will he eat his entire meal at one time. He will hide all the food that you give him, preferring to nibble on it all through the day.

Since the hamster is most active in the early evening, this is the best time to feed him. Establish a regular feeding routine and stick to it. In this way he learns that he is to be fed at a certain time and comes to expect it. One feeding a day is enough.

One of the advantages of owning a hamster is that he can take care of himself if you are going to be away from home for a few days. Make sure his water bottle is freshly filled or even use two temporarily and give him a large supply of dry food. He'll be able to manage alone for about a week.

In the desert, the native hamster obtains most of his water from leafy plants. He does not require much, but his water bottle should be kept filled with fresh water every day. If you have to move the feed dish, always return it to the same spot. Hamsters are creatures of habit and anything out of order displeases them.

Hamsters like living food too. They have been known to eat ants, sowbugs, cockroaches, flies, even hornets. So if you have any of these available, use them for food occasionally— live if possible.

Fresh fruit and vegetables should always be washed thoroughly before they are offered. They may have been

Another new color, not fully accepted, is Cinnamon. Similar to Golden, it is richer and glows with an orange cast.

Golden-banded and Cinnamon-banded. In this side-by-side photo, the differences in shading are readily apparent. The placement of markings is similar.

Male Golden Piebald. The spots should be distributed evenly all over the body and head.

sprayed with insecticides which are harmful to hamsters. Nor should more fresh food than can be consumed in a day be fed. Spoiled food or sour water (to say nothing of milk) can result in intestinal disturbances.

A few don'ts concerning hamster feeding: They should not be fed any of the acid fruits like oranges or grapefruit. Nor should they be given needles of the evergreens, either as food or bedding. Raw meat should be avoided too. It appears to encourage cannibalism. Garlic they don't like and onions will make them furious.

5   Taming your hamster

A new hamster is a nervous hamster. Make things easy for him when you first bring him home. Make doubly sure that no one frightens him with sudden movements or loud talk. It is wise to let him completely alone for the first few days unless he shows without prompting his desire to be friendly.

If your hamster arrives in a box, open it carefully. You will probably find him burrowed down in the litter. Do not thrust your hand in suddenly. He is more than likely to nip it. Let him first see the back of your hand. Then slip it firmly around his shoulders, so that the head lies in the palm facing the wrist. Quickly place him in his cage which, of course, you have prepared in advance according to the instructions given under *Housing*.

Make sure that his water bottle and feed dish are full and leave him alone, observing him if at all, from a distance, remembering always that hamsters have a sensitive nervous system and that strange sounds and voices will only terrify them.

Only when he has accepted his surroundings and set up housekeeping, so to speak, should you attempt to become acquainted. He will make his bed, establish his pantry, and choose a corner for his "bathroom". The female is usually more fussy about this than the male. He is inclined to be lazy.

Taming is a simple procedure. It is only a matter of gaining your hamster's confidence. He is, by nature, a gentle, friendly pet and you, too, must be gentle, friendly, and patient. Patience is particularly important. If you try to hurry things, you will only frighten him and have to begin all over.

First put your hand into his cage slowly. Offer him a tidbit: a sunflower seed, a peanut, or a raisin, holding it in the palm of your hand. Although he may seem shy at first, his natural curiosity will overcome his nervousness, and he will come over to investigate and then start nibbling. Now try stroking him gently.

When you sense that he is friendly enough to be picked up, do it in the manner described above; lift him out of the cage and place him on a table. Watch him closely, however. Hamsters have poor vision, and yours might walk right over the edge. Like most ground dwelling animals they have no instinctive fear of falling. A hamster is not able to turn his body in mid-air the way cats can, so a fall can hurt him badly. Pet him now and then and talk to him softly, using his name —yes, hamsters learn the sound of their names.

Do this as often as possible until your hamster gets completely used to you. The next step is to place your hand and arm on the table so that he can climb up it and onto your shoulders. Don't worry that he will fall off. Hamsters feet are well adapted to climbing and he is in no danger unless you make a sudden movement.

Next, unless you have a dog or cat, you can put your hamster on the floor and allow him to wander around. Keep a close eye on him, however: remember that he is small and can crawl into tiny spaces, and that you may have trouble finding him again. Remember too that hamsters like to gnaw so keep your eye on the furniture.

The Golden Hamster is, generally speaking, a submissive pet, but he will, on occasions, become unruly, possibly to impress on his keeper his courage and freedom from inhibition. Biting is a natural reflex when any animal is frightened or startled.

Any bad behavior can result from discomfort in his digestive tract, unclean or uncomfortable bedding, or illness. It can also be the result of noise or excitement, too much handling, or handling by a stranger.

An owner who is nervous about handling his hamster and always uses gloves to do so will soon discover he has a vicious pet. On the other hand, a person who is unafraid, who

This is a poor quality Piebald because the body spots are light and scattered.

likes animals and treats them with gentle firmness will have no trouble at all. Apparently hamsters can detect fear through their sense of smell, and fear causes a man to perspire. This perspiration scent is what causes the hamster's irritability. And when so aroused he will scamper about, turn on his back, bare his teeth, voice his war cry, and act belligerently.

Such animals can be gentled within two or three days if an unafraid person gives them special attention, quieting their fears and suspicions.

SALLY ANNE THOMPSON
From the Piebald, breeders are attempting to develop a golden face which would have a clear white body and a golden head.

6 Training

Once your hamster has become completely tamed, you can start teaching him to do tricks. Having a pet that can perform is a never-ending source of delight as well as pride.

Patience, perseverance and repetition are the keys to success in the training of any animal, hamsters included. How well you are able to train yours depends on how well you apply these three keys and on how much imagination you can bring to the training process.

The use of a reward is extremely important. This reward should be a treat that your particular hamster really enjoys, perhaps a peanut, raisin, or a bit of fruit. Hold it above his head high enough that he will have to stand on his hind legs to reach it. Repeat his name and the command "Stand" until he does, tease him for a moment and then give him his reward. Repeat this procedure and the command again and again until he stands whenever you hold your hand over his head, even without the reward. He will soon come to associate the word "Stand" with the act of standing up and do so whenever ordered.

Other commands can be taught in the same way, always remembering to repeat the identical word and procedure. By this same method you can teach him his name. Hold a bit of food out to him and call him by name. He will come for the food, and after a number of repetitions he will begin to understand that the name refers to him.

There are no short cuts to training. As we said before patience and perseverance are the keys. If you fail at first, don't be discouraged, don't say "My hamster's too dumb", but keep on trying until you succeed. Your hamster, like any animal, can learn only through constant repetition. If you try to hurry the process, you will only make him nervous and the training that more difficult. Be gentle, keep your voice low, and don't give up.

It may take time, but the result will be worth it. Console yourself too with the thought that after the first trick has been learned, the next ones will come easier and easier.

A hamster playground

Hamsters love to play and if you implement this natural playfulness with a playground you will find yourself spending many happy hours watching their amusing antics.

There are a great many toys on the market especially designed for hamsters. Parakeet toys are good for them too. We have already mentioned the exercise wheel. Most new hamster cages come equipped with exercise wheels, but if yours does not have one, or you have built your own cage, buy one at your pet shop. They are not expensive and home-made ones do require a certain amount of skill. If the cage is large enough, you may keep the wheel set up in it permanently; if not, set it up outside when you bring your hamster out to play. He will use it often, sometimes for an hour or more at a time.

Hamsters will also run up and down a ladder. One can easily be constructed with coathanger wire and two light sticks. Drill matching pairs of holes 1½ in. apart in these sticks. Cut the wire into 3 in. lengths. Force these into the holes to form rungs. Sandpaper any rough edges.

To make your hamster a slide, first construct two of these ladders about 16 in. long. Cover the lower half of one with plain smooth board, cutting it so that it completely covers the rungs; tack it securely in place. Angle the two ladders together in an inverted V and wire them securely at the top. Anchor the slide so that your hamster can't knock it over and then watch him enjoy himself.

Another plaything that is really a "must" is the stick of wood to gnaw on mentioned earlier. This can be hardwood or fruitwood and can be stuck across his cage like a perch. Hamsters must gnaw to keep their teeth in shape.

Not only is it natural for hamsters to gnaw, it is natural for them to dig, and happy is the hamster who has a sandbox of his own. This need be no more than a wooden grocery box filled about a foot deep with sand. Surround the box with a sea of newspaper and let your hamster burrow to his heart's content—under supervision of course. Make sure he cannot escape.

7 Breeding your hamsters

Until hamsters were first domesticated in 1930, it was assumed that rats and mice had the shortest gestation period of any mammal, 21 days. But the female hamster breaks that record easily with her period of 16 days. She can have her first litter when she is only eight weeks old and then, if birth control is nonexistant, have a litter almost every month for the rest of the year, with an average of seven babies each time. In that same year, her children, grandchildren, great-grandchildren, etc. will start having litters. So within twelve months (and providentially, female hamsters rarely

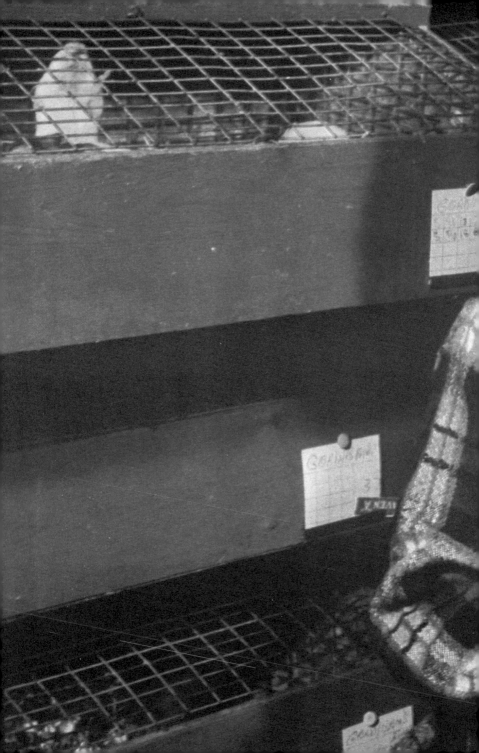

produce young after that first year) one pair of hamsters can, within the realm of remote possibility, generate one hundred thousand descendants!

Keep this figure constantly in mind if you decide to breed hamsters. Count the cages you will have to buy, the nest and cage litter, and the food. Breeding hamsters is not a field to be entered into lightly. So, unless you're ready, willing and able to take on a big job, better keep males and females apart.

Although the average hamster is capable of breeding when it is eight weeks old (some in experimental laboratories, have been bred at one month!) it is wiser to wait until the female is about three months old before mating her for the first time. She will then be better able to stand the strain of pregnancy and nursing her young.

In the wild state, hamsters have a definite mating season, but in the unnatural environment they are kept in as pets, *there is no season.* While they breed throughout the year, most litters are produced between May and November; in their wild state they are inactive and in semi-hibernation during the early spring and winter months.

The female's *oestrus* cycle (period of sexual heat) repeats itself every four days, but she can only be impregnated during the night of the first day. Since it is difficult for the novice to tell just when this time will occur, the simplest procedure to follow is to place the female in the male's cage for a period of no more than a week. This, however, is not quite as easy as it sounds. Many females will fight the male viciously. A careful introduction is necessary.

Never, but never, put the male into the female's cage. This is her home and she will attack at once in defense of it. When you have selected your breeding pair—and they should come from different blood lines, not be brother and sister—put the male in the female's cage and the female in the male's cage, but separately, not together at any time, until they get used to each other's scent.

Next return them to their own cages, but place the cages side by side so that they can get acquainted through the bars.

Only now, if they seem compatible, should the female be introduced into the male's cage, and it is wise to wear gloves when you do it. Because now is the time, if ever, that there may be a fight and you are standing by to separate them if it occurs. If the female is *not* in heat, such a fight is almost certain. The only time she will show affection is when *she* is ready to mate.

If she is ready, she will probably go rigid, tail up, head held low. They will both start running around the cage with occasional stops to examine each other's genitalia. When the female finally decides that the male is acceptable she will crouch and await his attentions.

But if a fight ensues, return the female to her cage and try again the next day. Some breeders claim that a young female finds an older male more compatible.

This introduction, perhaps we should have pointed out earlier, should only be done at night. Being nocturnal animals, hamsters prefer to do their mating then. Observations in laboratories have shown that most matings occur between nine and ten p.m. Eastern Standard Time; after eight p.m. Central Time; after six p.m. Pacific Time.

If immediately on the first meeting, no mating occurs, but they accept each other peacefully, it is safe to leave them together in the same cage until you are sure that they have mated. This may take a week but no longer. At the end of the week, if you are not certain, remove the female to her litter-cage anyway and wait to see if she shows signs of pregnancy. Four days after removal, place the male outside her pen. If she is aggressive, she is pretty sure to be pregnant; if she shows affection, she has still not mated.

When the female is about to be placed in her litter-cage, a nest box should be provided. This should be about six inches square with a small opening just large enough to admit the pregnant female. Excelsior, straw, hay or shredded paper should be provided for nesting material, but this should be placed in the outer cage. She will want to build her own nest. Do not even look into this nest until nine days after her litter is born.

During her entire pregnancy she should be left alone as much as possible. Keep cage cleaning to a minimum. Add milk to her diet (preferably powdered), see that she gets more green vegetables and, of course, as much water as she wants. This added diet should continue until she has weaned her young.

The birth of the young usually occurs at night. You can anticipate it if you know the exact time of the impregnation. It will be exactly 16 days, give or take a few hours, later. The

Male Golden-banded. This is a well marked hamster.

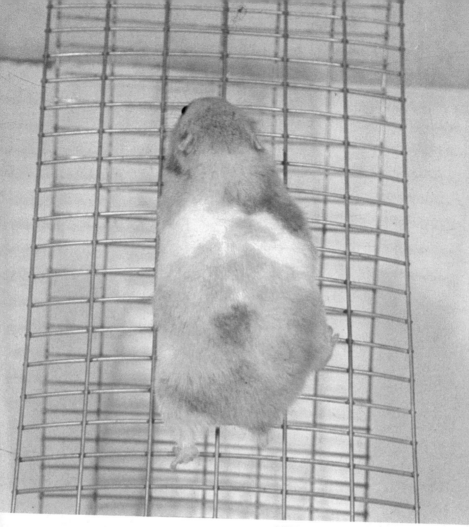

Breeders are attempting to develop a tricolored hamster, as seen in this female, fawn, tortoiseshell and white.

newborn hamsters (which you probably won't see because they are in the nest and it is inadvisable to look into it) are about an inch long and weigh less than an eighth of an ounce. There can be any number from one to a dozen, even more occasionally, but the average is seven. (If a female gives birth to less than seven, it is probably unwise to use her again as a breeder.) The babies are born naked and blind. They need no particular care, and should be left entirely to the mother.

Warning. Don't even touch one except in an emergency. The mother, resenting the new smell from your hand, is more than likely to destroy the baby. If for any reason you do have to touch a baby, touch all in the litter so that they will smell the same.

For the first nine days after birth, the little family should be left completely alone except for feeding or the removal of a dead animal. Only then should cage cleaning be resumed.

We do not recommend it, but for the record: if you are really in a hurry for hamsters the female may be bred again four days after the birth of her litter. She should, of course, be returned immediately to her first litter and kept with them until they have been weaned.

Although at birth the babies are blind, their teeth are already formed, and the body develops rapidly. By the time they are three days old their hair begins to grow, and on the fifth day the ears open. When they are eight days old, although their eyes are still closed, they will come out of the nest and wander around the cage, going to the toilet and eating the solid food which their mother will offer them. Once they do start eating, be sure to increase the dry rations.

The hamster mother, if she takes care of them at all, will take excellent care of her youngsters until they are two weeks old. Don't be surprised if she seems to swallow her babies; she is hiding them from some seeming danger.

However, the novice breeder should realize that some hamster mothers are cannibalistic and will devour their young, including the ones who die of malnutrition. This seems to be particularly true of first litters. It cannot be attributed to any one factor. It may be caused by unusual noises, strange caretakers or voices, by inadequate quarters or unsanitary conditions. If a female should destroy both her first and second litters, it is unwise to breed her again.

Sometimes females die when giving birth. This is because

of a malformation of the pelvis which is common in runty females. Only well developed vigorous animals should ever be used as breeders.

By the time the babies are two weeks old they will have a fine thick coat of fur and will weigh three times what they did at birth. Hamsters do not open their eyes until they are two weeks old. At the end of their third week, they should be weaned. At this age they resemble their bright-eyed parents and should be treated as adults.

When they are five weeks old they should be separated according to sex to prevent premature breeding, but each sex can be kept in a community cage until they begin to fight among themselves. Then they are ready for breeding. Remember, though, not among themselves. Keep introducing new bloodlines if you want big healthy litters.

Sexing Hamsters

Hold the animal in the palm of your hand on its back. The penis of the male is about $\frac{1}{4}$ to $\frac{1}{2}$ inch from the vent. The vulva of the female is closer to the vent and is mostly bare except for a few greyish hairs. The general body contour is also an aid. The male presents a tapered, elongated rear, while the rear of the female is more blunt and not as brightly colored as that of the male.

A quick breeding summary

Period: Will breed throughout year; most litters between May and November

First Possible Mating: At 43 days

First Possible Litter: 59 days; average 73 days

Mating Time: Introduce female to male after 6 30 p.m. Mating is immediate if female is in heat

Oestrus Cycle: Repeats every four days; impregnation possible only on night of first day

Gestation Period: 16 days

This particular male was a nervous individual and kept trying to escape. This is the wrong way to hold a hamster as it can easily fall.

SALLY ANNE THOMPSON

A hamster can go off a table top faster than you could believe. He should not be allowed so near the edge.

Number of Young in Litter: 1 to 15; average 7

First Solid Food: 8 days

Eyes Open: 14–15 days

Weaning: 18–21 days

Caging: Separate young males from females at 35 days

8   The genetics of hamster breeding

To understand why hamsters have different colors, and how to breed for these particular colors, we must turn to the science of genetics and its law of heredity. This natural law was first expounded by the monk Gregor Mendel in 1865 but it did not become generally known and accepted until 1900. Genetics, sometimes called Mendelism, is the study of how offspring inherit features, traits and color from their parents and grandparents.

It is sometimes difficult for those who have had no training in biology to understand Mendel's law. But explained in everyday English it is not difficult and it is what I will try to do now.

The reproductive cell of the female is called an ovum or egg, that of the male, the sperm. When sperm penetrates ovum a new individual is conceived. Each parent contributes half of its hereditary genes. Genes are like tiny packages of coded information, linked together in strings of beads called chromosomes. They are always paired *except* when the ovum or sperm is being formed. Then the chromosome splits in two lengthwise, and divides the hereditary genes in half. Half the mother's hereditary genes are in the ovum; half the father's are in the sperm. They meet in the impregnated ovum. A baby is on its way. The newly formed chromosome contains the detailed blueprints of its heredity: half from one parent, half from the other.

Now Mendel noticed that when he crossed tall garden peas with dwarf peas, the offspring were not medium-sized peas as one might suppose, but were *all* tall. The genes (or blueprints) for Tall had taken precedence over the genes that blueprinted Dwarf; they *dominated* them, and that is how the term *Dominant* used in genetics originated. The weaker blueprint for size, Dwarf, receded into the background—it was *recessive*. It was still there; it just didn't show. It was, shall we say, dominated by its twin.

And this explains why, many times, hereditary traits skip a generation. Many naturalists had wondered about this, especially in the case of human beings, but no one could figure out why until Mendel came along.

When he bred that second generation of peas (the ones that *looked* tall but came from tall and dwarf parents) he found that the new pea vines were *not* all Tall, that one out of every four were Dwarf. There were still, however, no medium-sized pea vines in this third generation. Just Tall or Dwarf; nothing in between.

When the Dwarfs of this third generation were bred together their offspring were *all* Dwarfs. When the Talls were bred together, however, the expected didn't happen. Some of the Talls produced only Talls but some (the hybrids) produced Dwarfs. Mendel worked out the mathematics of it: 25% Dwarf; 75% Tall *but*—and a very important "but"—of that 75%, one-third would be dominantly Tall and the other two-thirds (50%) would look Tall but they would be carrying the recessive Dwarf genes.

Now let us forget about Mendel's peas and see what happens when we apply his findings to hamsters.

Let us substitute for the Tall pea, the Golden color of the hamster; and for the Dwarf pea, the complete absence of color in the albino hamster. We will call the golden color, because we now know from long experimentation that it is dominant, *Solid Gold*. We shall call the recessive genes which produce the pure white hamster *Pure Albino*. We shall call the combination of dominant Gold with recessive Albino *Hybrid Gold*. Because albinism is recessive there can be no such thing as a hybrid Albino.

Let us assume that each mating gives birth to eight baby hamsters. There are six possible combinations that can turn up in that litter of eight.

SALLY ANNE THOMPSON
A Golden Hamster, startled at his meal, crouches and sounds his shrill warning. When cornered, a frightened hamster will throw himself on his back and bare his teeth. If undisturbed for a few minutes he will relax and become his normal friendly self.

A hamster's skin is very loose-fitting. He doesn't seem to mind being pulled up by the scruff. Should there be any danger of his biting, it's best to grasp him close to the base of the head. The skin of the shoulders is so loose that he can turn around in his own skin.

1. If both parents are Solid Gold, the eight children will be Solid Gold.

2. If both parents are Pure Albino, the eight children will be Pure Albino.

3. If one parent is Solid Gold and the other Pure Albino, the eight children will be Hybrid Gold.

4. If both parents are Hybrid Gold, of the eight children there will be two Solid Gold, two Pure Albino, and four Hybrid Gold.

5. If one parent is Solid Gold and the other Hybrid Gold, of the eight children there will be four Solid Gold and four Hybrid Gold.

6. If one parent is Pure Albino and the other Hybrid Gold, of the eight children, four will be pure Albino and four will be Hybrid Gold.

These averages will probably not, of course, appear in any one particular litter. They have been derived by counting a great many litters and arriving at these figures. Nor is it possible to tell which of the golds are Pure Golds and which Hybrid Golds. They will all look the same. But the Solid Golds will throw only Solid Golds. The Hybrid Golds will throw both types of gold as well as Pure Albino.

Mutations

All this being true, you may well ask, if each parent passes its hereditary traits on to its offspring with such mathematical precision, how can there ever be any new colors, features, and traits. What about evolution?

The answer is that in some way still not known to science the genes for form or color are changed in one parent, and these new genes are passed on to the offspring. Such a sudden change is called a *mutation* or, if it is a very dramatic change, a *sport*. Mutations are produced when a gene is so changed that it results in an inheritable trait: a change that breeds true and can be passed on to its children and grandchildren.

Do not confuse mutation and hybridization. A hybridization is a change that results from mating two different species or varieties and may not breed true or even be fertile. It is what we might do if we were to breed Solid Gold Hamsters to Pure Albino, get Hybrid Gold; interbreed them and get Solid Gold, Hybrid Gold and Pure Albino all in one litter. If we had bred Hybrid Gold but thought we were breeding Solid Gold and discovered a Pure Albino in the litter, we might jump to the conclusion that Albino was a mutation since both its parents were golden but we would be wrong. It is not a mutation; it is a hybridization.

It is now time to consider the many varieties of color in the so-called golden hamster, all mutations and all breeding true. We must keep in mind, of course, that almost all of these new color genes are recessive, and that the normal wild "golden" color is dominant.

Mutations

There have been numerous reports in recent years about new mutations but it has been impossible to confirm many of these. The following list includes only those that have been accepted by hamster authorities at the time of this writing.

Albino: The entire coat is pure white down to the roots, and devoid of any shading or marking. The eyes are a bright clear pink. The ears are flesh-colored and devoid of any dark patches. The gene is, or course, recessive.

Piebald: Also known as Pandas, Spotteds, and Harlequins. This was the first mutation to be discovered. There is an irregular pattern of white spotting scattered over the entire body with a characteristic white blaze on the face. The amount of spotting varies from almost none to more than

SALLY ANNE THOMPSON

This tortoiseshell hamster female has a mixed litter, showing their mixed ancestry. Disturbed at first by the box being moved, she hides under the lid.

Normally inquisitive, she comes out to investigate and to protect her youngsters which are about 5 days old.

SALLY ANNE THOMPSON

Confidence restored, she is ready to explore the world. The babies squirm around in an effort to get away from the light.

50% of the body surface. Eyes dark except if located inside a white fur area; this causes them to be pink. Animals with one pink and one dark eye are possible. Black or gray ears. Congenital deformities sometimes accompany the gene which is recessive. The mutants appear to be more nervous than normal hamsters.

Cream: Also known as British Cream or Ruby-eye Cream. Discovered in Britain in 1948. This factor produces a general dilution of all colors, affecting both hair and skin. Lovely creamy-apricot fur, paler on the underside. The dark pigment is prevented from developing in the hair but not in the skin, so that ears and eyes are dark. Black or ruby eyes. Some claim these are difficult to raise because the males become sterile and the females are inclined to be delicate.

Amber-Gold: Also known as Cinnamon or Champagne. Discovered by Blanche Hakes in 1958. The color is startling: a bright cinnamon-orange and the eyes glow a claret-red. Black pigment seems to be entirely lacking, producing the ricn orange coat. Ears are grayish pink, and while the eyes are colorless at birth they deepen in maturity. The normal black flashes at the cheek are changed to brown and the gray base of each hair is lighter than normal. The gene is recessive.

White band: The white band mutation was found about 1957. To be ideal there should be an unbroken band about an inch wide completely encircling the hamster's midriff. In practice, however, the band is sometimes wider, sometimes narrower, but it is always sharply defined. The ears are pink at birth, but in the adult only the bases of the pinnae (outer ear) remain without pigment. The rest of the ear is black. In some banded animals there will be scattered brown spots along the mid-dorsal line. Eye color is normal. The gene is dominant.

White belly: A single gene, partially dominant, produces a hamster with a pure white underside and slight dilution of eye color, so that while the eye appears black it glows a fiery red. If both parents contribute this single mutant gene, the result is a baby with all white fur, pink ears and eyes. The eyes, however, are extremely small and the lids remain closed resulting in a mutant known as the Eyeless White or Blind Albino. White bellies can be bred by crossing any hamster with a Blind Albino.

Black-eared Albino: Also known as Polar. This is not a true albino because of the dark ear color; in all other respects, however, it is, having pink eyes and snow white fur. The eye and ear color both darken with age. This mutation was first discovered in 1957. The gene is a single, recessive factor inherited independently of ruby-eye, cream, or piebald.

Black-eyed White: This is not a true mutation. It is a combination of the White belly and the Cream resulting in pure white fur, devoid of any marking. Dark ears and eyes. It is not an Albino although sometimes called that.

Other but less well known hamster mutations include the Mottled White which is sex-linked and results in a sparse coat of golden and white fur on the back; Tawney, the shade of a lion with dark eyes and ears; Woolly Pink which has a pink-toned fur with a curling tendency, and Silver, Gray, and Blue—this last very rare. Cream Panda is not a mutation but a combination of Piebald and Cream.

It may be wondered if there are many other mutations still undiscovered. It is possible, of course, but not too likely. Remember that all new color variations are not the result of mutations. Some have come from simple crossbreeding—the Piebald and Cream resulting in the Cream Panda. Remember, too, that the entire genetic storehouse of our present-day hamsters goes back to that single litter discovered in 1930.

No doubt we will continue to hear new reports because of the mounting interest in scientific hamster breeding. It should be realized, however, that the evidence required by a geneticist for a new mutation is far more scientific than that by the novice fancier.

Nevertheless, if an unusual hamster does turn up in one of your litters and you are only a novice, report it at once to someone truly interested in color genetics so that the strain may be perpetuated before it disappears. This has, unfortunately, happened in the past with the result that some mutations have been, perhaps forever, lost.

9   Your hamster's health

A clean dry cage is essential to your hamster's health. He does not like dampness; he will suffer from it. A hamster kept in a small dry cage that is changed often will remain in better condition than one kept in a large cage in which moisture, especially urine, is allowed to accumulate.

Do not put water in a cup for drinking purposes. It is almost certain to be spilled into the bedding material. Do not allow fresh fruits or vegetables to remain in the cage uneaten. They too can contribute to the unwanted dampness. If bedding does become wet for any reason whatsoever, replace it immediately with dry litter.

Be sure that wild rats or mice do not have access to your hamster's cage. They are carriers of all kinds of parasitical infection. If you purchase a new hamster make sure that he is in good health before bringing him into the same room with your others.

Household pests like roaches, bedbugs, and mites frequently enter hamster cages. When using an insecticide remove the hamster from the cage—a glass jar with a wire screen cover can serve as a temporary home—and place him in another room. Disinfect the cage thoroughly, discarding all old litter, replacing it with new, and do not return the hamster to the cage until you are sure that it is perfectly dry.

Hamsters are rarely attacked by mites or fleas, but if this should happen, commercial sprays are available. Do not use any spray prepared for dogs on hamsters; cat sprays are permissible.

Hamsters are susceptible to drafts and they do catch colds—human colds and other respiratory infections—so if any member of the family is suffering from one, he should not handle the hamsters or even enter the room in which they are housed. If your hamster does come down with a cold,

SALLY ANNE THOMPSON

An alert little animal, the hamster "freezes" at a strange sound. The whiskers are sensory organs, and help him find his way through dark tunnels.

and you have more than one, he should be immediately isolated from the others. Again, a wide-mouthed jar with litter on the bottom and wire netting taped across the top can serve as a temporary "hospital".

The hamster's cold symptoms are much like yours: runny nose, sniffles and a general "under the weather" behavior. When he ignores you when you call him for meals it is a good sign that something is wrong. Make sure that his cage is in a warm, dry place, and cover it with newspapers or fabric to keep out drafts. See that he gets fresh water and give him a little cod-liver oil. A couple of drops on a piece of bread is enough. Clean out all old litter and replace with new. Do this again after he has recovered to prevent reinfection.

The best way to tell if something is wrong with your hamster is to compare his present behavior with normal behavior. A healthy animal, on wakening—do not expect this liveliness during the bright hours of day—will run around his cage, wash himself, stand on his hindlegs, and climb the wire walls of his cage. His fur will be clean and smooth and he will carry his short tail erectly. Listlessness, dull eyes, no appetite, rough coat, and general emaciation are all negative indications.

The hamster's teeth are his greatest weakness. They break off, acquire cavities, and are subject to decay. However, hamsters do have one advantage over us poor humans, their teeth keep growing. That is why it is wise to keep a branch of hardwood like oak or walnut in their cage to keep the teeth worn down.

Broken teeth resulting from falls or biting wire can result in an inability to eat and malnutrition if not outright starvation. If this happens, adjacent teeth should be clipped with heavy duty nail clippers so that they mesh easily with broken teeth and enable the animal to eat.

Examine your hamster's teeth regularly for cavities or signs of unusual discoloration, wearing gloves, of course. If a tooth is loose, you can probably pull it out with your fingers, staunching the blood with a bit of gauze held firmly. If a tooth is in bad shape but not loose, let a veterinary pull it.

Many times a hamster's dental problems can be solved by adding more milk to his diet. This can be fed in his water dispenser or by feeding bread and milk, or, and preferably, using dry milk. Care must be taken that the milk does not go sour, and that milk-soaked bread is not hoarded.

If your hamster is caged by himself, there will rarely be any cuts, wounds or bites to worry about. Hamsters in community cages do fight, sometimes to the death, and that is why keeping them together, even by sexes, after they have matured is not recommended. As to wounds, there is no need to be concerned if the hamster can reach them with his tongue; his constant licking will prevent their becoming infected. Otherwise, treat them with a mild antiseptic like tincture of merthiolate applied with a cotton swab. Do not bandage the wound. If it is bleeding freely hold a bit of gauze firmly against it until the blood clots. A wounded hamster should never be kept in a cage with others. They are likely to attack him.

The hamster's droppings are a good clue to the state of his health. If they are rod-shaped of normal consistency all is well. Loose, watery droppings indicate too many fresh fruits and vegetables. Hard dry droppings indicate not enough. Constipation is more common among young hamsters; make sure that they get plenty of fresh water.

Wet tail

Here is a hamster ailment, the exact nature of which is not understood. Old and young are susceptible to it. They become emaciated and weak, and the area around the anus becomes wet and discolored as if the hamster were suffering from diarrhea. Its cause is not known, but the current assumption is that it is the result of a diet deficiency. The natural food habits of the wild hamster are little known. There is, perhaps, some vital dietary component found in their native habitat that scientists have not yet discovered. Even perhaps a living food, like a live insect. Improper cage-care may also be a factor, particularly allowing stored food to decay, or the bedding to remain damp.

Cage paralysis

Another disability related to improper diet. The hamster becomes inactive, cannot raise his head, and moves along pushing its nose on the floor. This results from a lack of Vitamin D and not enough exercise. Cod-liver oil will supply the needed Vitamin D. Feed it on a piece of dry bread.

Mites

If your hamster's coat has a moth-eaten appearance accompanied by skin irritation it may be due to mites. Commercial sprays are available for this. Use cat not dog sprays.

While runny eyes are the sign of a cold, they can also indicate food stuck in one of the cheek pouches. Use a small medicine dropper to flush the pouches with warm water. This is why it is unwise to give soft sticky food to a hamster. Irritation and ulceration can result.

This Cream hamster likes crackers and cheese. A little, as a treat, is fine but too much will cause problems.

Be extremely careful of falls. A fall from the door of the cage or off a table, or even out of loving hands, can often prove fatal.

On each hip hamsters have a tiny gland which secretes minute quantities of a fluid something like musk. They spend much time preening the fur around this gland just as birds preen their feathers. It does not mean that anything is wrong.

Hibernation

This can happen if the temperature drops. You may think your hamster is dead. He will feel cold to the touch and lie still in your hand. Warm him gently with your body heat. Carry him around with you cupped in your hands. Feed him warm milk from a medicine dropper, one drop at a time. Pick him up from time to time, warming and rewarming him. When he revives and you return him to his cage, better cover the cage with heavy cloth.

Since the hamster is such a remarkably healthy animal, chances are that you will not be faced with any of the above ailments. If something does go seriously wrong and you are not able to handle it with any of these treatments, isolate the hamster at once and consult your veterinarian. A really sick animal will, perhaps, have to be destroyed.

0 The scientific use of hamsters

The European and Chinese hamsters were used for laboratory experimentation before the Golden Hamster was discovered in 1930. The Chinese hamster was first used experimentally as far back as 1919.

The first laboratory use of the Golden Hamster was in experiments to discover the mode of transmission of the serious tropical disease known as Kala-azar, caused by the bite of a sand-fly. Before then Kala-azar was almost always fatal. Today, thanks to the Golden Hamster, 90% of all cases are cured.

Since then Golden Hamsters have been widely used, according to Rae Whitney of the Bio-Research Institute at Cambridge (Mass), for parasitological and bacteriological studies and have, in addition, become useful as experimental hosts for viruses such as those of poliomyelitis, canine distemper, mumps, blue tongue of sheep, equine encephalitis, Colorado tick fever, herpes simplex, equine abortion, influenza, rabies, and others.

Because of its ability to develop tooth decay under induced dietary conditions, the hamster is used a great deal in dental research.

Since they hibernate in response to cold weather, they are well suited to studies of natural and induced hypothermia and its effects upon mammalian physiology.

The hamster's cheek pouches have given scientists a living laboratory for the study of microcirculation. By using blunt forceps to avoid injuring the membrane, these pouches can be pulled from the animal's mouth while under anesthesia and stretched over an illumined stage for observation, thus forming a living laboratory for the study of tissues. Many studies on tumor growth have been done by using one of these pouches as an implantation site.

The reproductive processes of the hamster have had a great deal of attention because of its unusually short gestation period of 16 days as well as the remarkably precise timing of the female oestrus cycle.

Hamsters have long been employed in nutritional studies, and in quick tests for human pregnancy.

Note: Neither the Department of Agriculture nor any other unit of the US Government recommends raising hamsters as a source of large profits. Nor is it advisable to raise many hamsters before making arrangements for marketing the surplus animals to some hospital, laboratory, biological supply establishments, or other institutions. Most of these organizations buy their hamsters in such large quantities with specified delivery dates that it is impossible for the small breeder to supply them.

There is, of course, a small market available in local pet shops, and in schools, supplying hamsters for science projects.

1 A cautionary warning

CAUTION

The US Department of Agriculture has issued the following warning:

> Breeders of Hamsters are cautioned to prevent the escape of any of these animals. Such release under favorable conditions might establish the Hamster in the wild and thereby create a serious rodent problem, since they are destructive to growing crops, gardens, and other agricultural enterprises. Purchasers should be aware of the danger of escapes, and make every effort to prevent the establishment of a wild colony.

2 Hamsters: The pet for everybody

No other pet is better suited for living in your home than the furry and friendly hamster. He is clean, gentle, quiet, and cuddly—a playful little animal whose antics will provide hours of fun for the whole family. What makes him an ideal pet is that, unlike so many other pets, he requires little space and almost no care; all he needs is a loving owner.

Children as well as grown ups find that hamsters make interesting playmates. Give a hamster an appreciative audience and he'll perform his best and show his most acrobatic scamperings. Give a child a hamster and you have given him a little friend with whom he can spend many happy hours.

And if you give your child more than one hamster, you will have started him on his way to a worthwhile and informing hobby. Breeding hamsters is easy, owning two hamsters is twice the fun of owning one, and the study of their life cycle is fascinating.

Young hamsters of different color varieties are being raised together. They are all of the same sex to prevent fighting. The wooden containers are lined with wire screening because the hamster is a growing animal.

SALLY ANNE THOMPSON